Hints to cadets, with a few observations on the military service of the Honourable East-India company

Captain Thomas Postans, Thomas Postans

HINTS TO CADETS,

WITH

A FEW OBSERVATIONS

ON

THE MILITARY SERVICE

OF THE

HONOURABLE EAST-INDIA COMPANY.

———

By LIEUT. T. POSTANS,

BOMBAY ARMY.

———

LONDON:

Wm. H. ALLEN AND CO.,

7, LEADENHALL STREET.

1842.

TO THE

HONOURABLE COURT OF DIRECTORS

OF

The East-India Company,

AS A

TOKEN OF THE MOST RESPECTFUL GRATITUDE,

THE

FOLLOWING FEW PAGES

ARE

DEFERENTIALLY INSCRIBED,

BY

THE HONOURABLE COURT'S

MOST OBEDIENT AND VERY HUMBLE SERVANT,

THOS. POSTANS,

Lieut. & Assist. Political Agent, Upper Sindh.

a

INTRODUCTION.

As the military service of the Honourable
East-India Company must be interesting to
a large portion of the British community,
whose relatives find in it a valuable provi-
sion, combined with honourable distinction
to all whose zeal or talent renders them
deserving the approbation and patronage of
the Government they serve ; and as, at the
same time, the circumstances connected with
the early career of the Indian Cadet are
little, I believe, either understood or appreciated, as affects their various bearings upon
his future prospects, I have been induced
to throw together the following hints and

brief opinions, as the result of personal experience during my own period of service in the East, and I now submit them to the reader, with that humility but sincerity of purpose which should ever wait upon a difficult but interesting subject.

SHIKARPORE, *Aug.* 1841.

HINTS TO CADETS,

&c.

CHAPTER I.

EDUCATION, AND PERIOD OF QUITTING EUROPE.

To fit men for every position of life in which they may be placed, it would seem profitable and advantageous that the education of each individual should have reference to the particular interests and objects of their future career, as, in any other case, much that is valuable will remain unlearned, and on that which is relatively useless, much valuable time may be squandered. For professional life in England, a peculiar and distinct system of education is considered necessary to fit the young aspirant for the Church, the Bar, or the practice of the Medical art;

and even in a lower grade, the father who
desires his son to adopt any particular trade
or calling, invariably decides on an education
calculated to fit him for its distinctive duties.
It is, I believe, an acknowledged fact, borne
out by observation, and to be illustrated by
examples, that the fortunes of an individual
are materially within his own power, and that
few have in early life set before them the
desire of attaining a particular object, and
directed their aim and energy towards its
steady attainment, without, sooner or later,
meeting their reward in success.   Certain
means will commonly produce certain ends,
which, under the usual routine of events, may
be calculated upon with tolerable security;
and surely if this be admitted as a truth, it
affords sufficient incentive to constant and
well-regulated exertion, whilst, setting aside
the responsibilities of man in the discharge
of his individual duties to his country and
himself, few are so dead to the excitements
of ambition as not to desire the gratification
which springs from power, and the applause
which waits upon a distinguished position

earned by individual merit. In the naval or military professions, the liberal education of a gentleman is added to by the particular studies which more especially bear upon the discharge of the duties belonging to either service; and it must be evident to all who have studied the histories of the heroes of our country, that even while events arose which led to the full developement of talent, and those so highly distinguished became so perhaps by the force of circumstances; that yet, the means must have previously existed, by cultivation and energy, to enable those individuals to grasp at the occasions which fortune cast within their reach.

We commence, therefore, by admitting as truths, that the acquirement of a distinguished position by personal merit is a decided good, and the legitimate object of that ambition which is, in a greater or less degree, implanted in the nature of every man; and we allow that this good may be attained by the application of means adapted to the end, and a steady perseverance in the pursuit of the object proposed. It will consequently result, that the points to be considered in connection with these subjects are, first, the character and nature of the profession on which a young man is about to enter, and, secondly, the particular views therein which his studies and preparations should be calculated to advance.

Between the Military Service of the Honourable Company and that of the Royal Army there are wide distinctions as respects the positions and duties of the officers serving therein ; the Military profession generally, it has been remarked, requires in its aspirants the liberal education of a gentleman, with the addition of those studies calculated to form the officer and soldier. These are a necessary and indispensable portion of the Cadet's preparation, be his destination for either service, but in that of the East-India Company are involved responsibilities and peculiar duties which have elsewhere no parallel, requiring an unusual degree of intelligence for their due discharge, whilst in India there is no limit to openings for the exercise of useful and practical knowledge, the field of exertion and distinction being at the same time accessible to all who exert themselves.

The aspirant for the honour of serving in India will consequently find his own best interests, no less than those of his country, seriously involved in giving a due degree of attention to qualify himself for the field of action on which he is about to enter before quitting his native country, and, by arriving at just conclusions as to the position he is about to occupy, comprehend fully the various obligations he will therein be called upon to fulfil.

Before proceeding to offer such remarks as may conduce to the above desirable ends, I would wish to be understood as addressing myself to those who, as parents and guardians, are fully alive to the advantages of the service in which they are about to place their charges, and anxious for their welfare therein; as also to Cadets who are disposed to use every exertion, and attend to any suggestions calculated to ensure their future success, having arrived at that age when advice is

duly valued, they having, moreover, a just
appreciation of the noble calling on which
they are about to enter—in the very best
military service in the world.

An error is, I am of opinion, generally
committed in sending Cadets to India at
too early an age, under the idea, I presume,
of its giving them some advantage in promotion, acclimation, or habituating them to
the country and the service. Leaving these
for the present, the following reasons are
offered for dissenting from this system, and
I should say, that twenty will be found far
preferable to the age of sixteen or eighteen,
at which boys have been in the habit of
leaving England.

In the first place, it is next to impossible,
in sending the Cadet fresh from school to
India, that the discipline of his mind, as
respects moral character and steadiness of
purpose, can have been matured (a highly
necessary and more important point, as I
shall hereafter shew, than is generally considered); and, again, his education, though it
may have been all that the best of public or

private schools can give him, is not of that
description, and does not embrace those particular subjects, which are essential to his
success in India, coming under the general
denomination of useful, practical knowledge,
acquired only at an age when it can be understood and appreciated from its relative
value.

Without, however, entering into farther
argument against the too youthful entrance
of the Cadet into the service, I would rather
proceed to point out the advantages of his
being of a mature age before he quits his
native country, and how the intermediate
time may be most profitably disposed of;
with other remarks bearing on the subject.

We will conclude that the Cadet of the
present day (for the service has taken a decidedly higher stand as respects the class of
society entering it of late years) has re-
ceived the liberal education, say of our public schools, and if at Addiscombe, that he
has there made himself acquainted with the
theory of his profession; taking him to be
thus at the age of eighteen as emancipated

from school and college, there would remain, under my plan, two years to be filled up, previous to his final departure for his destination—valuable time, every hour of which may be turned to the most profitable account if rightly employed.

The great desideratum in India being practical knowledge, and the military service offering not only no impediments to the exercise of such, but, on the contrary, the Government holding out every possible inducement to such of its servants as possess the necessary qualifications, the opportunity should be seized by the Cadet of availing himself of the facilities afforded in the present day for acquirements, which will be immediately brought to bear in a country where the field of inquiry is boundless, and whose geographical features and extraordinary physical resources are yet but partially developed, though daily becoming of greater interest, and attracting the attention they merit. I would instance geology, mineralogy, mechanics, surveying (in all its branches), as of the greatest value, and political economy, with every point of information which may lead the possessor to statistical and geographical inquiry. These do not ordinarily form a portion of school education, nor are they, indeed, attainable except under circumstances, and with that degree of undivided attention which they require. Their value to the possessor will soon be apparent, as I shall proceed to shew, and the time I have allotted in England for their acquisition will be well employed, and any expense or exertion amply repaid.

Having before alluded to the encouragement held out by the Indian Government to the capable portion of its servants, I may point out as an example the Bombay army, the smallest of the three presidencies of India, furnishing, from its twenty-six infantry regiments of the line alone, about one hundred officers holding staff or other appointments independent of regimental duty. In these situations are comprised the whole of the quarter-master-general's department, trigonometrical and revenue surveyors, assistants to mint engineers, superintending operations of boring for water, repairers of roads and tanks, assistants to engineers erecting public works, and other posts, not one of which can be held but by scientifically qualified officers, but offering at the same time the best proof to be adduced of the premiums given to talent by Government, and shewing that the wants of India call for a constant supply of qualified men from its army, to take upon them offices of trust and responsibility, apart from the regular outline of mere military duty.

It would doubtless be out of the question to expect that a young man should enter India at twenty as a completely accomplished character, or that his acquirements should embrace all the increased scientific knowledge of the present day; my object is rather to point out, that by delaying the Cadet's departure until the above age, and directing his studies from the time of his quitting school until that period to subjects such as have been mentioned, he will have the greatest possible advantage over the mere inexperienced youth, in promoting his

own advancement, and will not fail to have
his qualifications sooner or later called into
action. Let him, therefore, though he only
obtain such ground-work or theory as may
be perfected by practice hereafter, still adhere to the plan I have proposed, and make
the best possible use he can of the time allowed him. But to use another argument
in favour of the value of resources and interesting studies in India for which a taste
has been imbibed at home, I must observe,
that the nature of the climate and military
duties in India, admit of abundant leisure,
a commodity, according to its employment,
either of the highest value to its possessor,
or proving, as is too often the case, his bane
and greatest misfortune. For nearly twelve
hours daily, the military man in that country is master of his own time, for the prin-
cipal part of the year a prisoner in his own
house, and entirely dependant on his own
resources. Happy the man who has such at
his command, though they be of the lightest
kind; but when there exists the power to
turn the time thus placed at his disposal to

useful and profitable account, its possession
is a positive good; and this will be accomplished by the Cadet's acquiring the groundwork of such objects of study as have been
before alluded to, combining at once powers
of resource and means of advancement.

I may here remark, that I consider much
labour and valuable time as wasted at home in
the study of Oriental languages as a means
of qualification for India; the end proposed
is in the first place not answered, for the very
trifling knowledge which can, after all, be
acquired, is of little or no actual use to the
student, who in England invariably finds the
thing distasteful and difficult from its *outré*
style and character; a few months in the
country (India), with association and the
necessity of circumstances, will place the
Cadet in possession of all he requires for his
immediate purposes; and for prosecuting his
attainments further, due time and attention
are alone required. I shall allude to the
study of languages in India hereafter; at
home, the mind should be directed to points
and objects only there to be obtained, with

this reflection, that the Cadet, on departing from his native shores, leaves the very centre of civilization and the fountain of human science behind him, and that he will have reason to congratulate himself hereafter if he has availed himself fully of the same, and is prepared for his exile by a due stock of acquirement; but that if he neglect the opportunity, it can never be recalled.

There are also no refined or manly accomplishments without their utility in India, the former as resources, the latter as sure to be constantly called into action—these are also indispensable to the soldier; but of accomplishments, I would instance music and drawing as worthy of every cultivation where the taste is found to exist. As previously mentioned, want of occupation to fill up time is the bane of Indian life, and all legitimate means should be encouraged to counteract it. For the pencil, India offers probably a wider scope than any other country in the world, in the grandeur of its scenery, interesting beauties and peculiarities of its architecture, picturesque costumes, and

striking characteristics of its various races.
Drawing, independent of its employment as
an amusement, may be made subservient to
the most valuable purposes in India, and
add greatly to the reputation and advancement of its possessor.   Let the Cadet first
experience for months the dull and dreary
monotony of solitary outpost duty, as assuredly in the course of some he will, and
he can then fully appreciate the inestimable
value of having the wherewithal to get rid
of intolerable *ennui* by either of the above
means, in a position where many men have
for want of them sunk under it, and sacri-
ficed themselves at the Indian Moloch of
dissipation.

There is a hackneyed, but not generally
and sufficiently understood expression connected with our rule in the East, *viz.* that it
is one of "*opinion ;*" as it bears materially
upon, and is intimately connected with, our
subject, I shall observe, that by it must be
understood, that we govern the millions in
India by means of a high moral estimation
formed of us as a nation by the natives of

the country, which has had the result of attaching to us and our interests an army of 250,000 men from amongst themselves, in whose fidelity we have trusted and must trust for retaining possession of our vast territories, whilst the whole machine of government, and discipline of that army, are in the hands literally of a mere handful of Englishmen. The Cadet destined for the Indian service need, therefore, scarcely be told that he must, under such peculiar circumstances, occupy a most important, prominent, and responsible position, as a representative in his own person of his country, and that the obligations and duties which will be imposed on him individually are of no ordinary kind.

By permitting the Cadet to attain a sufficient age before he finally quits his native country, to allow of his having seen and mixed as much as possible with the world, he will be enabled to meet with judgment and forbearance those trials to his prejudices, habits, and tastes, which he must undergo amongst a strange people, who are powerfully prejudiced themselves, and who keenly feel and deeply resent any encroachment or want of attention to their immemorial usages and customs. The natives of India are eminently acute, observant, and correctly judging, with an extraordinary discrimination of the characters of those placed over them, highly susceptible of considerate treatment, and always to be gained over by mild rather than by other means. The English officer in India, being in constant communication with, and having to command a people of this character, should have his mind well schooled to regard them leniently, and not to condemn because at first he may not be able to understand; he being bound, moreover, by every consideration of duty, apart from all others, to induce every feeling of attachment and respect to him, and through him to his nation, as a link in the chain which binds India to England. Such results will be obtained, if the Cadet shall have combined with his education that formation of character and those habits of thought, the result of travel, and an extended view of society and human institutions, which come with mature age.

With the mere schoolboy, suddenly freed from all restraint and sent to India without judgment or experience to guide him, the converse of what I have sketched is too often the case; he struts a man without any other apparent object but that of shewing his right to assume the character, which he imagines will be best done by venting his ebullitions of temper on his servants and the natives generally, annoying the native soldier by a fierce demeanour, and want of all consideration for his feelings and peculiarities. He dislikes and despises the natives because he cannot understand them; they are, in his opinion, an inferior order of beings, to whom he is under no sort of obligation to pay the slightest respect, and he thus contracts habits of violence which never quit him, and a prejudice against the people and country which adheres to him through life, making his position one of constant annoyance, at the same time effectually preventing his proving either a profitable servant to the

Government, or capable of advancing his
own interests. Native troops, moreover, like
others, do not feel that respect which in-
duces obedience, when they are commanded
by mere boys, and the general effect is therefore bad as respects tone and discipline;
but when considered in the light of heavy
responsibility attached to individual servants
of a government, holding millions in subjec-
tion solely by the force of opinion, or a high
estimation induced in the minds of the subjects, from the comparatively few examples
of the conquerors whom they see amongst
them, it becomes of paramount importance,
that each and every aspirant for the Indian
service, particularly the military, should have
left all the trifling actions and ignorant conclusions of boyish years behind him, and enter on his career with a mind fully prepared
for its importance, and well schooled to the
thoughtful mood and reflective habits of
mature years and riper judgment.

It will conduce materially to just conclusions respecting our rule in India, and to a
knowledge of the fundamental principles on

which we exercise our sway in that vast
country, if the Cadet should seek every opportunity of studying the various works conveying information on these subjects, as also
by availing himself of the experience of those
who have served in the East, and who have
it in their power to enlighten him on much
which it is highly important to him to know.
Forming as he does part of a system where
the responsibility is, to a certain extent,
shared by every servant of the state, the
more extended his acquaintance with the
economy of that system, the more efficiently
will he be enabled to perform the part allotted him. The sooner he acquires this insight into India and Indian affairs, the better; on his arrival in that country, his inquiries will be advantageously directed to
fill up the outline which he has thus obtained in England.

The nature of the service, expenses at-
tendant on carriage, &c., do not admit of a
young officer's possessing an extensive collection of books of his own; and in the
present day, there are fortunately few of the

Indian stations unprovided with a library, or
few well-regulated messes without its book
club; still the general taste inclines towards
light reading, and I may therefore suggest
the few following works as valuable companions, and in every way worthy of finding
a place amongst the other "necessaries for
a Cadet."   Indian Despatches of the Duke
of Wellington and Marquis of Wellesley;
Gleig's or Mill's History of India; the former,
as published in the Family Library, is more
portable, though incomparable to the latter
as a standard work; Malcolm's Central and
Political India; and the Lives of Munro,
Clive, and Hastings.   There are of course
numerous other works appertaining to India
which might be mentioned, but the list is
too long, and I therefore particularly recommend the above, as calculated to convey
every useful historical and political information, as also to illustrate, in the lives and
actions of the great men who have raised
themselves to the highest pinnacle of fame
in India, what has been and may be again
achieved in that country by adhering to cer-

tain rules of conduct, and prosecuting with vigour the opportunities there presented for distinction. I shall sum up these few remarks by particularly recommending to the Cadet's notice the example of Sir Thomas Munro as to the footing on which he placed himself with the natives of India, and the estimation in which he held them; and by directing his attention to the method of economizing his time, as exemplified by all the great men whose names I have alluded to, for on this and its duly profitable disposal depends entirely his advancement in India no less than elsewhere.

The rapid communication now opened with India has, fortunately for the Cadet of the present day, superseded the necessity of his undergoing the tedium and monotony of a four months' voyage round the Cape, where, independent of complete waste of time, intolerable *ennui* and its concomitants drive young men to various methods, all more or less highly objectionable, to get rid of the annoyance. Gambling is, or was, the general resource, leading in most cases to violent

conduct between the parties; courts-martial,
as a consequence, greeted the Cadet's arrival
in India, and even before he had entered on
his career, he found himself in bad odour
with his superiors, and a stigma was attached
to his character, calculated to act most un-
favourably to him hereafter. Such things
have repeatedly occurred in outward voyages,
and therefore their recurrence, as a possibility even, is to be avoided. Let the Cadet
by all means avail himself of the overland
route, and he may, by extending his travels to
some of the capitals of continental Europe,
lay up, under proper guidance, a store of
useful information and pleasing reminiscences
for the future in their languages, institutions, &c.

One great advantage, however, of approaching India by this method is, the mind becoming gradually accustomed to an Oriental
people, scenes, and customs, thus avoiding
that sudden and great change experienced
when transported at once from England to
India, and the great distaste to the latter
consequently experienced from the sudden

transition. On the other hand, the Cadet will approach India somewhat prepared for what would otherwise appear to him strange, uncouth, and annoying. In a word, no additional argument need be wanting after those already given to the world by various great authorities, as to the enlargement of mind resulting from travel, when combined with observation and reflection. To the Indian Cadet I would distinctly say, that his time, thus employed, is well and profitably disposed of. Let me instance the antiquities of Egypt: much as these have excited the admiration and wonder of the world, they excel only in their stupendous character the superb cave-temples, granite sculptures, and ancient fanes of India; but the contemplation of the former will doubtless excite a taste for similar monuments of past ages in India, of which they are alone the undying chronicles. Here is at once an inexhaustible source of study and inquiry, of the most engrossing and interesting description, and the Cadet may reflect, that he will have it in his power to add his name to the list of those great men who have added to our knowledge of India as the most ancient and interesting country in the world, viewed in her religion, and its monuments, language, and social institutions.

Alluding to any advantage it may be supposed the young man will have in point of health by being early acclimated to India, I would observe, that such is not proved to be the case from experience, but, on the contrary, a certain maturity of constitution would appear far better adapted to the climate than otherwise. I would instance the assistant-surgeons of the Honourable Company's service, who are not allowed to enter it until they have attained the age of twenty-two; yet, considering the trials of constitution to which they are exposed in the discharge of even their ordinary duties, they have, I should say, rather the advantage in point of health over the other members of the service; and, looking at the subject statistically, it has been lately strongly recommended, that European recruits for India should be allowed to attain the age of twenty or twenty-one, on account of their decidedly superior stamina, and consequently less liability to suffer from the climate at starting. I may add, also, in the case of the officer as in that of the soldier, that they are found to avoid those dissipating habits into which the younger fall, and which are far more to be dreaded, and far more fatal in their effects on the European constitution, than the much though unfairly abused tropical climate. On this head there is certainly nothing gained, and therefore no argument in favour of quitting England at so early an age.

Few better securities for rectitude of conduct and steady adherence to the duties of his situation can be found, than a knowledge by the Cadet that his career is watched with the deep anxiety and interest of valuable friends in his native country; such associations as he shall have formed with men of learning, worth, or science during the period he is pursuing his after studies and acquirements, will, in this way, be of intrinsic value, for that man will be likely to prove a keen guardian of his own honour and reputation

c

who knows that he is an object of scrutiny to persons whose opinion he values and respects; and this will be another and not trifling advantage of a protracted stay in England.

To his country and all its associations he should ever feel the strongest attachment, and studiously avoid adopting either Eastern habits, tastes, or customs, as degrading to him as a member of the most civilized nation in the world, hurtful to his character individually, and annoying to society at large, at the same time (though it may, by the uninitiated, be considered as paradoxical to say so) having the direct effect of lessening the respect of the natives of the country themselves towards him. Errors on this head, however, are not uncommon, though a little reasoning would prevent them. The natives do not give the adopter of their customs and habits any credit for other than sinister motives in his proceedings; whilst, by assimilating himself with and becoming one of them, he at once sinks all right to be looked upon with the respect which should attach

to him as their European superior, and he
experiences their contempt accordingly.

In concluding these remarks, I would simply call observation to their leading facts, all
of which, I believe, will be found calculated
to prove that a system varying from the one
in common practice, as regards the Cadets of
the Honourable East-India Company's service, might be followed with advantage, both
to the individuals concerned, and the service
to which they have the honour to be ap-
pointed.

The subject for consideration appears to
be, the propriety of a more advanced age for
the entrance of the Cadet upon his military
duties; and I have endeavoured to shew,
that by a wise and judicious application to
those studies calculated to extend his views,
and his being allowed to attain a certain
stability of moral character, he will be better
fitted for the discharge of his prospective
duties; and that the Cadet will find the in-
terval between his leaving school and arriving
in India one of incalculable value, if properly
employed; while his health will in no way

suffer, but that rather his constitution will be the better prepared to meet those changes to which it will be exposed in the climate of the East.

As I believe that the more these facts are considered the more their truth will be admitted, I shall leave them to the reader, without further intruding upon his attention that multiplicity of reasons which might be adduced in their support, did I feel that they required it, and proceed at once to the consideration of other points of interest to the young military man in the Company's service; and the first of these I consider to be the Native Army of India.

CHAPTER II.

NATIVE ARMY OF INDIA.

THE history of the world does not present a more extraordinary or interesting political phenomenon than the position we hold in India. A rich, vast, and thickly populated country, its inhabitants composed of distinct races, following various creeds and usages; warlike tribes, who will bear comparison with any in the world in physical stature and determined bravery—in short, few portions of the earth present such a diversity of inhabitants, whether considered morally or physically, as British India. Yet is this vast machine guided and kept in perfect order by what may be literally called, a mere handful of Englishmen; a number, in short, so disproportionate to the masses governed, that it is as nothing; moreover, the great instrument used to effect this apparent impossibility is an army of 250,000 men, raised from the inhabitants of the governed country, modelled and disciplined in every respect to form an integral part of the British army, whose fame its brilliant achievements have on all occasions tended most materially to enhance.

" By the natives we conquered India, and by them we must maintain it," is the opinion of Sir John Malcolm, than whom few who have treated on the native army of India were such perfect masters of this important subject, or so well able to handle it. In all the features of the British supremacy in India this is certainly the most interesting, and, to the Cadet, a point to which his inquiries and attention should of course be assiduously directed.

There are those who, in their enthusiasm for the native troops in India, accede to them all the qualities of the soldier possessed by his European brother in arms.   Physical

capabilities, however, in the first place, and
the acknowledged superiority of the British
soldier over all others in the world, will not
admit of unqualified assent to this opinion;
but certain it is, that amalgamated with the
European soldier, and having his example
before him, there is nothing of daring courage or patient endurance that the native
soldier will not perform or undergo, as the
chronicles of our wars in India will fully
testify, his attachment to his officer at the
same time amounting to a devotion, where
the proper pains are taken to foster it.
Though apparently the most apathetic of
human beings, the native soldier is, on the
contrary, highly excitable, and more keenly
alive to the interest felt in him, or otherwise,
by his superiors, than a superficial observer
would be disposed to believe. The peculiar
characteristics and striking qualities, however, of this class of men, on whom we are
solely dependant for our retention of British
India, having been elsewhere so ably and
fully discussed, by those whose authority is
incontestable and of weight in such matters,

I shall rather adhere to general instructions for the Cadet's guidance in his intercourse with the native soldier, and the means to be adopted to keep up that steady attachment and fidelity to our interests, for effecting which the European officer is responsible to his government as its immediate agent, since it is obvious, that an army chosen from the people of a conquered country, and employed as the means of keeping possession of that country, must be a delicate engine of power, requiring nice judgment and constant care, so as to combine firm adherence to our interests with the strictest submission and obedience incidental to discipline and effective order. These great objects are, and have been, alone effected by a high standard of qualification, on the part of the European officers, for the important trust committed to their charge.

It has been a fundamental rule in our Indian administration, not only to exercise the most unequivocal toleration towards the natives of that country, but also to abstain most scrupulously from any interference in

their cherished prejudices, whether social or
religious: with the native army, this is most
rigidly adhered to, and though the Cadet, on
first entering the service, will not fail to per-
ceive from the practice of others that such is
the case, he may yet inadvertently offend in
this important point entirely through ignorance. To obviate this, therefore, I would
strongly recommend his losing no time in
making himself acquainted with the leading
and distinctive marks of Hindoo or Mahomedan prejudice, so that in his early intercourse with the natives generally, and particularly the troops, he may not create the bad
impression which on this account too often
attaches to the new comer, avoiding, at the
same time, the infliction of unnecessary pain
to others.

It might be supposed that the striking
difference of religion, immutable laws of
caste, customs, habits, and great national
discordancies between the European and
native of India, would, singly or collectively,
offer insuperable barriers to that community
of feeling and degree of attachment which

are essential between the soldier and his
officer to ensure mutual confidence, and
therefore discipline and efficiency; but such
is not the case; for though, it is true, we
know comparatively little of the natives of
India generally, from the impossibility of our
seeing and mixing amongst them when freed
from all restraint, and in their own social and
private intercourse, yet the native soldier,
having no real home for the greater portion
of his life but his regiment, and being entirely
dependant for his comfort and success in his
career upon his officer, is brought more immediately in contact with us than any other
class of natives; and with those who study
his feelings, and interest themselves in his
welfare, there is not the most trifling circum-
stance, connected with his private affairs
even, on which he will not consult his European officer, whilst he courts his attendance
at his festivals and holidays as a high honour.
The lengths to which the native soldier will
go, in defiance of the most cherished and
deep-rooted prejudices of religion and caste,
can only be fully appreciated by those who

know how nicely sensitive he is on these
points; yet the instances are of daily occur-
rence where he loses sight of and incurs the
penalties of loss of caste, and sacrifices his
most darling attachments to the laws of his
religion, all in favour of his officer; 'tis he
indeed who can induce the sepoy to go to
any extent for the service, and it may be in-
ferred, that when discontent or any thing
approaching to a mutinous feeling is shewn
amongst the native troops, something radi-
cally wrong between them and their officers
will be found to exist, so that the latter have
not the confidence of their men.

I have said enough to prove that the distinctions between the natives who serve in
our Indian armies are fictitious as applied to
them and their European officers; the Cadet
should therefore study to banish from his
mind any preconceived notions which he may
have imbibed to the contrary, and be fully
prepared to meet the native soldier as he
would his fellow-countryman placed in the
same relative position, — to treat him, in
short, with the consideration and frankness

due to a loyal and faithful servant of his country, and by evincing an interest in and regard for his comfort, welfare, and respectability, induce an attachment which, whilst it acts most beneficially in securing the fidelity of these gallant men to the British Government, never fails to reward the British officer with a devotion in time of need unsurpassed by that of any other soldier in the world.

The sepoy, in common with the natives of the East, having peculiar powers of discrimination, and observing the characters of their superiors with remarkable scrutiny and just conclusions, it becomes highly necessary that the European officer should study to preserve that high tone of moral conduct which alone can gain respect for him among a class remarkable for habits of the strictest sobriety, temperance, and order, and in whom a departure from these principles in their superiors never fails to excite the strongest feelings of contempt.   Another point on which I would particularly remark, is the necessity for the constant practice of mildness of demeanour,

coupled of course with firmness as occasion
may require, in the intercourse of the European officer with the sepoy under his command. Natural impetuosity of temper, together with a want of an acquaintance with the
language and customs of those with whom
he communicates, frequently lead to a violence of expression and harshness of tone
highly unbecoming to the officer, considering
the position he holds, and never failing to
excite the most unfavourable sentiments
towards him in the mind of the native soldier, who is thus addressed and treated as an
inferior being, whilst he, in fact, by the constant display and practice of some of the best
qualities required in a military subordinate,
deserves the highest consideration and kind
treatment from his superiors.   All these are
the common errors of men young in years
and new to the country and service ; but as
they are calculated to produce evils of the
worst kind, it becomes eminently desirable
that the education of the Cadet should be
calculated to soften and rectify them, and
that the European officer, from the moment

he enters the service, should be prepared to recognize the peculiar high qualities of the native character, apart from circumstances of religion, colour, or custom, as also determined to shape for himself a course of that moral, rational, and correct kind, which, whilst it is observed by the intelligent and scrutinizing people around him, shall secure from them that approval on which the respect of the native soldier to his officers will alone be founded.

Prejudice is the universal companion of limited views, and a residence in the East, if the individual concerned possess but a common degree of observation and intelligence, seldom fails to remove all erroneous opinions connected with the natives of India, particularly those in our service, and to supersede them by just views of their real worth and value as a people; and though this is usually the result of time and constant intercourse with those amongst whom his lot is cast, combined with the study of their language, histories, and customs, yet, as it is to the Cadet I am addressing myself, I would

wish to give him the advantage of avoiding
at the outset the great evils to himself and
the service which want of information on
these points might otherwise cause him to
commit.   Let me add, in the words of Sir
John Malcolm, "I must here remark, that
I have invariably found, unless in a few
cases where knowledge had not overcome
self-sufficiency and arrogance, that in propor-
tion as European officers, civil and military,
advanced in their acquaintance with the language and customs of the natives of India,
they became more sincerely kind to them;
and, on the contrary, ignorance always ac-
companied that selfish pride and want of consideration which held them light or treated
them with harshness."   I shall consider it
unnecessary to say more on this subject than
to remark, in connection with it, that, keenly
alive though the native soldier be to his laws
of religion, caste, &c., he is at all times ready,
nay pleased, to see the European officer
evince any anxiety to become acquainted
with them, and will never be found back-
ward in affording information to the inquirer.

The native commissioned officers of the
Indian army are a class of public servants of
whom our nation may be justly proud ; raised
from the ranks after long periods of unde-
viating fidelity to the state and good conduct
as soldiers, they demand, not only on this
account, peculiar respect from the European
officer, but being, at the same time, the immediate agents of his authority, they must
possess his complete confidence in the discharge of the many important duties dele-
gated to them.   They fill up the blank left
in our native regiments by the small pro-
portion of officers (European) to each, as
compared with the royal and other armies.
Moreover, as the commission is the summit
of the native soldier's ambition—the reward
to which he is taught to look for long, faithful, and steady service performed, the European officer should studiously evince in his
intercourse with this class of men the high
estimation and respect in which they are
held by him, and through him by the British
Government.   To the Cadet I would observe,
that on all occasions, when visited by a native

officer, even on duty, he should treat him as an equal, and accede to him all the courtesy due to him as such.

The experience of the native officers, or all connected with the service and country, will be found of great value to the young officer, and he will only require to evince the slightest disposition to cultivate their acquaintance, to procure all the information they are so well able to communicate. I know of no better or more direct method of winning the favourable opinion, at the out-set, of these old soldiers, than by demanding some account of their services. It will not fail to strike the observer, that on no sub-ject they dilate on these occasions with so much warmth, as the names of those dis-tinguished men who have rendered our arms in India illustrious, under whom they have served, and by whom they have been com-manded; on the memory of these the na-tive officer dwells with a warmth of feeling not to be mistaken, affording a striking proof of lasting attachment and respect.

There is a most important point, however,

connected with the native commissioned officers of our Indian army which must be strongly borne in mind, *viz.* their immediate influence over the men, and the power which they thus possess to prove the most useful or the most dangerous servants of the state : they have ever proved the former, and it is only requisite in the European officer, as indeed his paramount duty, to treat this highly meritorious and respectable class of men in a way to ensure their self-respect and attachment to the service ; this done, we may rest assured, from past experience, that our confidence in the native officers of the Indian army will not be misplaced.

I must impress on the young officer about to join the Indian army, that its history, probably beyond that of any other, furnishes some of the most striking instances of chivalric courage and high daring on the part of individual British officers ; and the peculiar constitution of that army, the native soldier taking his example entirely from his European superior, will always render it necessary for the officer serving with native

troops to be prepared to place himself fore-
most in times of danger. The sepoy must
be led, and when led, few indeed are the
instances where he has not nobly and de-
votedly supported his officer, particularly
where there exists a personal attachment,
induced by generous treatment and a mutual respect.

At the risk of repetition on so important
a point, I shall conclude this part of my
sketch by remarking, that, as a representative of the British nation, let the young man
destined for India adopt invariably a kind-
ness of manner and a conciliating tone in
all his intercourse, not only with the native
troops, but natives of the country generally,
he will find them a mild and inoffensive
race, though by no means an inferior order
of men; on the contrary, did my subject admit of my entering on the question, it could
be shewn that the natives of India demand
our respect as a highly intelligent and won-
derfully capable people. I have quoted
high authority to demonstrate that extended
acquaintance with and · knowledge of their

customs, language, &c., will be alone required to induce a highly favourable opinion of and attachment to them. I would, however, ask the Cadet, whether the generosity of character peculiar to his nation, apart from all other considerations, does not sufficiently point out that it is far more becoming, and indeed imperative on the British officer in India, to study to improve and elevate the moral characters and conditions of those who, by the force of circumstances, have become subjects to our rule as conquerors, than to continue a line of conduct calculated to depress and abase them? It must, moreover, be borne in mind, that if he aspire to hold any important or responsible office from amongst those open to him in the country of his adoption, the Government will not fail to require as a special qualification, that his habits and intercourse with the natives should be free from violence of temper or disposition, and marked by consideration and interest in their peculiarities. I trust I have said enough to guide the Cadet in the outset of his career on points where it is particularly imperative upon him to dismiss all prejudice; I alluded to his extended system of education as calculated to bring this desirable object about, and I have repeated the argument here, coupled with certain rules and information for his direction.

If he require further proofs beyond those I have adduced of the estimation in which the native army of India is held, and of the degree of consideration which the native soldier merits at his hands, I would only refer him to the ample testimonials afforded in our Indian annals, and the opinions entertained on these points by some of the best generals and most enlightened statesmen the world ever saw.

I shall now proceed to make a few remarks on such of the languages of India as are of immediate use to the military officer in that country, with suggestions, the result of experience, on their attainment.

CHAPTER III.

LANGUAGES OF INDIA, AND REMARKS ON THEIR ACQUIREMENT.

THE dialects of the vast Peninsula of India are no less varied than the countries and people composing it, and offer continued subjects of interest and study to the Indian officer who would dip deep into philology. For the immediate purposes of the Cadet, however, there are only one or two which demand his early attention, and to those he had better apply with as little loss of time as may be. They will be found to offer only such impediments as are readily to be surmounted by ordinary application and colloquial practice; and though the subject should not be viewed as a formidable under-

taking, yet certainly as of immediate importance to the Cadet, for he can be of little
use to the service, and will at the same time
continue to suffer the greatest personal in-
convenience, until he possesses at least the
power to make himself understood on the
ordinary topics connected with his wants
and communications with the natives of the
country.

The universal language in use in the army
is the "*Oordhu*," or language of the camp,
better known by its title of *Hindostanee*,
from its obtaining in great purity in Hindostan and the upper provinces of India and
Bengal. This dialect being universal with
all natives who have been brought into contact with the European community, as also
the immediate means of intercourse with the
native troops, no officer can be considered
as of any efficiency in the service until he
obtains at least a sufficient knowledge of it
to make himself understood and convey his
orders. A few weeks, with ordinary application, will enable him to do this if he per-
severe in colloquial practice, and take but

the common precaution of avoiding attend-
ants who speak English. Let no consideration tempt him to adopt this idle, though
convenient method, often pursued by new
comers. It is the necessity of circumstances which will be found of so much use
in teaching the Cadet the required quantum
of Hindostanee, and he will be a gainer in
the end by sacrificing a little personal convenience at first to attain his object. I may
at the same time point out as a general rule,
that the servants who are *au fait* at English
smattering, and who attach themselves to
the Cadet on his arrival, are generally a dis-
honest class, whose services he is far better
without.

The grammatical rules of this language
are few and simple, and the Persian character, in which it is written, so easy of acquirement, that I cannot allow a Cadet more than
four months study with a moonshee, not only
to be a good colloquist, but to be prepared
to pass his examination before a committee,
and qualify himself for an interpretership.
This he should by all means effect as soon as

possible, for he has thus made the first step to advancement in the service.

Hindostanee, or *Oordhu,* as its signification implies, is a mixed language, being the Persian and Arabic, introduced by the Mahomedan conquerors of India, interwoven with the Hindee, Sanscrit, and other original languages of the country. A thorough acquaintance with it, whilst indispensably necessary, has the additional advantage of giving the possessor a good groundwork for the study of and an insight into other Eastern languages. The few books required in the Hindostanee (for it may be said to possess no literature) are pretty well known, though they will be mentioned hereafter for general information.

For the Bengal and Madras armies, Hindostanee may be said to be the only medium of communicating with the troops, and the language universally used in the army, and all over the country.

In the Bombay presidency, however, the ranks of the army being recruited to a great extent from the Mahratta country, that language is also in very general use, it being customary to explain the Articles of War, and other general orders, in Mahratta as well as Hindostanee. This language, though more comprehensive and idiomatical, will be found to present few difficulties after the attainment of Hindostanee; its grammar is equally, if not more simple, the printed character, or Dewa Nagri, is easy, being the same as employed in the Sanscrit, or original and ancient language of the country, and is given in most Hindostanee grammars. I do not wish to be understood as insisting on the immediate acquirement of Mahratta; on the contrary, it may be an after consideration.

As the officer whose lot is cast in the Bombay army will necessarily pass much of his service in the Deccan and other portions of the country subject to that presidency, where the Mahratta language is the only one spoken and understood, he will find it of the greatest advantage to make himself a proficient in it; for, independent of its use with the troops, it is essentially necessary as a qualification for many important posts filled by officers of the Bombay army. It is a more copious language than the Hindostanee, and the great means used at Bombay of conveying instruction to the natives. The works and translations in Mahratta are extremely numerous. An admirable dictionary has been published under the orders of Government, and a learned member of the Scotch Church and admirable Oriental scholar has produced the best grammar extant. I may remark, in speaking of this language, that it will be found a useful means of bringing the student into communication with learned pundits and Brahmins, and with its study he will combine a knowledge of the singular religion and customs of the Hindoos, which he could scarcely so readily obtain by any other means. These observations are of course only applicable to the Bombay presidency, in which the writer has served, and with which he is consequently more fully acquainted, than with either Madras or Bengal.

The Guzerat division of the Bombay presidency has also its dialect, known as *Guze-*

rattee, the character differing but slightly from the Devi Nagri, or Mahratta, it being of Hindee extraction. It is in general use amongst the whole of the trading and banking portion of the community at that presidency, as well as over a large extent of country in Kattaywar and the Guzerat peninsula. All accounts are kept in Guzerattee, and that energetic and clever race of men, the Parsees of Bombay, employ it universally, even to the transcription of their creed and forms of prayer. Although not of immediate use to the military man, it may become essentially necessary to him in the discharge of either civil or political duties on the Bombay side. After the Mahratta, its acquisition will be found a task of the easiest kind.

Under the Bengal presidency, the army being composed of natives of Hindostan, *Oordhu* or *Hindostanee* is the only dialect, as before observed, used by the native troops, and being the universal language of the country, is spoken with a greater degree of purity and grammatical accuracy than in

any other part of the peninsula. As it is on
that side of India more copious and more
interwoven with Persian than elsewhere, a
knowledge, to a certain extent, of this latter
is required from officers in public examina-
tions, as also of the Hindee or original
Hindoo dialect of the country. This latter
is, like the Guzerattee before described, the
communicating medium and the language of
accounts amongst the banking and trading
classes, its character being derived from the
Sanscrit. It obtains only in the Bengal and
upper provinces of India. Persian is the
language of the courts of revenue and jus-
tice, and the great communicating medium
of the educated and higher classes of native
society throughout the whole of the Bengal
presidency. A knowledge of it is an essential in the education of a respectable native on that side of India, as also an indispensable qualification for public employment
under our Government.

In the Madras, unlike the other two presidencies, the native languages are not, I
believe, in such general use as in the other

armies. English is much spoken and understood by the native soldiers, who here ap-
proximate more to European habits and
customs than in the other armies, the rules of
caste, &c., not being so rigidly adhered to.

On the southern peninsula of India, the
Carnatic, &c., there are numerous dialects
of the Hindoo languages, such as the Gran-
tha, Teluga, Karnataka, Malayalma, and
Tamizh; but these can only be objects of
inquiry and study after considerable advance
shall have been made in others, and their
acquisition is also connected with a desire
to obtain an extended knowledge of India,
its antiquities, and the ancient characters of
its languages.

Having thus briefly alluded to those languages or dialects which the Cadet will
find either in immediate use, or of immediate advantage to him in his position to
acquire, I shall proceed to remark, that if
he purposes extending his knowledge of the
country and establishing for himself some
reputation in the service, he cannot adopt
a more direct means of profitably occupy-

ing his time than by studying to become a
good Orientalist; by which I mean, not at-
tempting to obtain a superficial knowledge
of the innumerable dialects scattered over
the vast extent of India (these alone would
occupy a volume to describe), but restrict-
ing his acquaintance to those in common
use before alluded to, and making himself
at the same time as proficient as possible in
Persian and Arabic; I would say Sanscrit,
as the groundwork of all that is valuable in
connection with the Hindoo religion, and a
knowledge generally of that interesting people;
but as the attainment of even an outline of this language requires intense study
and undivided attention, I shall leave it to
the taste or inclination of the student, who
may congratulate himself on his perseverance, if he is enabled to get even an insight into this most difficult of dead languages.

The Persian has the following advantage
to recommend it to the student's notice over
other languages in use in India. It is exceedingly rich and melodious, copious, and

capable of expressing, as Sir William Jones observes, "the most beautiful and elevated sentiments," whilst its poetry and literature generally, particularly historical, will well reward the time and attention bestowed upon its acquirement. Again, it will be found of essential service to the possessor in his intercourse with intelligent Asiatics, being the language in use throughout the whole of the Mahomedan courts, in and beyond the Indian territories, and a vast extent of country beyond the Indus, and in central Asia. Our advance to Sindh and Affghanistan has particularly called this language into request. In these countries it is so universal, that few officers can be considered qualified for public employment without it, and no traveller can make his way to advantage without a practical knowledge of Persian. It will be sufficient to mention, that the commonest and most servile classes of Hindoos speak this tongue fluently in Sindh and the countries to the N.W. It is by no means a difficult matter to obtain a superficial knowledge of Persian for purposes

of ordinary conversation, &c., but to be at all
able to read and appreciate any of the works
of the best authors will require considerable
study, coupled with an insight into the composition of the Arabic language, since no
sentence in the former can be practically
or properly turned without an Arabic construction, and no well-written Persian work
is considered complete without Arabic cou-
plets and quotations from the Koran and
other works. Let the student, however,
read the admirable Introduction to Professor
Lee's edition of Sir William Jones's Grammar to obtain a correct estimation of these
two languages, and turn his attention, as
soon as he finds he has attained some insight into the peculiar genius of Oriental
tongues, to the acquirement of Persian, for
he will find it not only of the greatest utility
in the course of service, but a valuable
source of acquiring information, particularly
on historical points; whilst its poetry, ethics,
and fables, will afford a continued source of
amusement and relaxation. Persian is a necessary appendage to the European officer

who aims at being an Orientalist, or who pretends to any degree of acquaintance with Mahomedan history or people.

The following remarks on the study of languages in India are offered with all deference, but, as the result of experience, they may prove useful. The " organs of language " (as the phrenologist would say) are certainly more " prominently developed " in some individuals than others; the facility of acquiring them, in short, would appear to be a peculiar faculty, with which some people are gifted in a high degree, whilst there are those who, although not wanting in application and perseverance, appear to be totally deficient in the capacity of catching the idea of any other dialect or language than their own. Such cases are, however, very few, and I can safely say, for the Cadet's encouragement, that I never yet met with a young man in India, who sat himself down on his first arrival in the country, when his mind was vigorous and well attuned to study, determined to conquer a language, that he did not readily do so; and it most frequently happens that the attainment of one begets an ambition to be master of another, and thus examination succeeds examination, only to add new honours to the young officer's acquirements as a linguist. The season for this description of study, however, is immediately after the Cadet's arrival, and should never be allowed to pass unprofitably. He will, in the first place, have more time and greater facilities at his disposal then than hereafter ; application will not be so distasteful as it will be likely to prove after a residence of some time in the country, when, with all the means and appliances at his command, and notwithstanding the exertions to the contrary, a certain degree of inertia and lassitude, the effect of climate, will usurp the place of the vigour and elasticity of mind which the Cadet brings with him from his native country.

The grammatical rules of the common Indian dialects, though exceedingly simple, as before observed, are yet, in most of our grammars, represented under technicalities, which tend much to embarrass the student at starting, on a point where he should be

quite unconcerned ; for I consider the rea-
diest method to acquire the Indian languages
to be by speaking and reading, without reference to any knowledge of grammar beyond
the most simple rules, as, for instance, the
formation of the verb ; and when an insight
is thus obtained into the particular idiom or
genius of the language (if I may use the
expression), those grammatical rules which
would otherwise have been unintelligible, and
on which much time and labour would have
been spent in vain, will not only be divested
of difficulty, but become self-apparent. Taking Persian for an example, and the otherwise admirable grammar by Professor Lee,
being an improved edition of that by Sir
Wm. Jones, now generally in use, I would observe, that though this work is well adapted
and valuable to those who may have obtained
a degree of proficiency in that language, it is
totally unintelligible as an elementary work
and means of instruction to the beginner,
who may toil for months over its Arabic
terms to parts of speech, tenses, genders,
numbers, and cases, and other formidable

rules, without having made a single step towards a practical knowledge of the language
itself; whilst the same time bestowed in
reading easy stories and colloquial practice,
would have gained for the student a good
insight and groundwork upon which to advance farther.

I venture to suggest, therefore, that the
student, instead of setting himself down to
conquer the Persian grammar in detail, should
content himself with obtaining a pretty ac-
curate knowledge of the formation of the
regular verb in its ordinary tenses, as the
present, past, future, and imperative; and
couple with this the perusal of the simplest
stories he can procure; for which purpose I
know none better adapted for beginners than
those in "Gladwin's Persian Moonshee;"
these having the English translations in jux-
taposition, will enable him soon to acquire
an insight into the grammatical construction
and peculiar idiom of the language, the former being, if reduced to its simple rules, of
the plainest kind—a verb of one conjugation,
no declination or genders to the substantives,

the easiest possible form of substantives
when connected with adjectives, the irregular
verbs so few that they offer no difficulty ;
and, in short, as the only thing requisite to
obtain a practical knowledge of Persian is to
be acquainted with its idiom and the system
of affixing those particles which make up its
deficiencies and form its peculiarities, so this
will be best obtained by reading in the first
place, and then, as the student proceeds, consulting his grammar to fix the rules in his
memory.   As he acquires he will find an in-
creasing desire to know more of this language, and, by the time he is able to peruse
and appreciate such works as the "*Anwar i
Soheli*" (the famous fables of Pilpay), he
may, by reading alone, become a perfect master of the grammar and syntax, whilst those
rules of grammar and composition which
would otherwise have puzzled and embar-
rassed him sorely, he recognizes as simple and
self-evident.   On all occasions he should of
course seize every opportunity to converse,
however inaccurately he may express himself
at first.   Translating from English into Per-

sian the student will also find admirable
practice for grammar, and the best means of
procuring a good stock of words, since it
obliges him to consult his dictionary, and
thus affixes them more on his memory than
by any other method. Six months' ordinary
application of say four or five hours daily will
suffice, after a knowledge of Hindostanee, to
make a good practical Persian, though a long
period of study and reading may be necessary
to become an elegant scholar, so as fully to
understand and appreciate the classical literature (so to speak) of such authors as Hafiz
and Saadi. The same remarks will apply
(*mutatis mutandis*) to the other languages of
India: they should all be rather attacked *in
medias res* than by the slow progressive
methods elsewhere employed, particularly
where the facilities are so abundant for practice in the colloquial. Studying these languages in Europe may be a different matter,
and may require, from the absence of colloquial practice, a very different method; but
as applied to India, I have found the plan
suggested the best.

Arabic, to acquire moderately even, requires so much time and application, and involves the necessity of taxing the memory with so many rules, that the zeal of students in India generally evaporates with the heat of the climate, and the majority are contented to halt at Persian and the general outline of Arabic, which is intimately connected therewith. But I should wish to encourage the student, from the very fact of the absence of many Arabic scholars in India, to the study of that language, by pointing out the estimation in which it is held and the pains taken to acquire it by the learned men of Europe. It would be misleading the student, however, were I not to point out that years of steady application are requisite to master this tongue; but when mastered, it will amply repay all the time and labour bestowed upon it. The native grammar, or " *Mizau*," written in the Persian, is by far the most simple and comprehensive of any European translation or paraphrase, as also are the other rules for this language, as given by the native gramma-

rians themselves. After having conquered
Persian, an inclination to know something of
Arabic generally exists, and it should be encouraged.   Certainly all others sink into in-
significance when compared to it, either as
a means of extended knowledge or for its
own intrinsic value, as one of the most ex-
pressive languages in the world.   I must re-
peat, however, that as a taste for languages
is oftentimes observed to be a peculiar faculty in individuals, general rules can hardly
be laid down applicable to all who attempt
their study; still the opportunities and abundant facilities which the officer will find
in India, will at any rate leave him no ex-
cuse for not paying a considerable share of
his time and attention to a subject which,
to him and his prospects, as a public servant,
he will find of vast importance and an indispensable qualification ; whilst he can never
expect to attain any extended acquaintance
with the most interesting subjects of the
people of India, their religion, customs, or
antiquities, &c., without a knowledge of
their languages.

Connected with the few foregoing · remarks, the following list of works, adapted to the study of some of the languages of India in general use, may be inserted.

Hindostanee — Shakespear's Grammar; Shakespear's Dictionary. For perusal: *Bagh o Bahar; Totah Káhání.*

Mahratta — Dr. Stevenson's Grammar; Molesworth's Dictionary. For perusal: *Æsop Netee*, a translation of Æsop's Fables. There are, however, numerous admirable translations in this language well adapted to the student.

Guzerattee—Forbes' Grammar; and, for perusal, *Pauch o Packyan,* a collection of fables.

Persian—Persian Moonshee, or Lee's edition of Sir William Jones's Grammar, the former for the beginner; Richardson's Dictionary. For perusal: *Gulistan* and *Anwar i Soheli,* or Fables of Pilpay; the latter is the best Persian prose work extant.

Perusal of letters and petitions for practice in the *Shikusteh,* or broken running hand used in manuscript.

Arabic—native grammars; *Meezan, Soruf i Meer*, &c.

Kamoos' Dictionary, Calcutta edition; *Alif Leilah*, or Thousand and One Tales, as published in the original by Macnaghten.

CHAPTER IV.

GENERAL INSTRUCTIONS.

As I consider it incumbent on all who, from a long residence in India, have the means at their disposal, to give the uninitiated the advantage of that personal experience acquired in a country where so much depends on certain rules and habits of life, and where all hinges so materially on the sojourner's disposal of his time and energies, I purpose appropriating the following few remarks to points for the Cadet's information generally connected with India and a residence in that country, merely premising, that my opinions and hints are offered with due deference to other authorities, though certainly with the best intentions and wishes for the welfare and interests of those to whom they are addressed.

We will suppose the Cadet to have landed in India as a perfect stranger, locally, to the country, and all connected with the arrangements for his servants, living, and future disposal, and consequently liable to all those impositions and extortions to which he must, under such circumstances, be for a time exposed. Where the Cadet has not that greatest of all advantages at starting in India, *viz.* a constituted adviser in the shape of a relation or friend, bound to take the new comer under his protection, and see him safe on his career, the only alternative is, to make it a rule not to act in any one instance, even to the engagement of a servant or disposal of a rupee, without consulting some of the many old officers of the service at the presidencies who can guide him; and as the Cadet will be there attached to a regiment, he will have no difficulty in finding those experienced heads who will be happy to assist him with their advice and experience. It is a conceited idea of acting on his own judgment

and impulse which leads the Cadet at starting, not only to spend large sums of money
uselessly, but to be continually exposed to
the most bare-faced extortion, without procuring one particle of comfort, or being provided with a single article of use to him
hereafter. He is looked upon, under any
circumstances, as fair game by all with whom
he attempts to deal; and when he couples
with his total ignorance of all about him an
air of conceited reliance on his own discrimination, there is really, after all, little blame
to be attached to those who profit by it. The
servants who are in the habit at the presidencies of attaching themselves to Cadets,
and whose general recommendations are
comprised in an insufferable stock of impu-
dence and a smattering of English, are sys-
tematic rogues, who have no other object in
view but to rob their masters; and when,
by the time he quits the presidency for the
Upper Stations, they find his experience in-
crease, whilst his means of being any longer
profitable to them diminish, they never fail
to leave him unceremoniously, to pursue the

same system with the next new comer. These the Cadet should studiously avoid; they are well known, and no old hand would allow him to have any thing to say to them for a moment. Good and respectable servants are indispensable to the young man's comfort, no less than to prevent his being pillaged and imposed upon from other quarters; to obtain these, he should rely entirely on some other opinion than his own.

It is not my intention to enter into the details of what are required, in the shape of equipment in India, to place the young officer in a position to proceed to his ultimate destination, as these are points on which he will soon be fully informed on his arrival in India, but I would wish particularly to warn him against burdening himself with a single superfluity, and recommend his limiting his baggage to what may be called " light marching order;" he will find his advantage in this hereafter; above all, let him avoid, as he would his worst enemy, any extravagance which, exceeding his means, shall involve him in debt, even to the smallest amount;

debt, in any shape, is one of the rocks on which many a man has been shipwrecked at the very outset of his Indian career, and is fraught with so many considerations of moment and danger to the Cadet's future career, that he cannot keep it too often in view. He will find in India, at the presidencies particularly, unusual facilities for procuring money or obtaining credit, and the ease with which it is to be accomplished, with the many temptations and fascinating opportunities for availing himself of these means, are too apt to blind him to the consequences, and to spread a false colouring over the future; but of this he may be certain, that the day will most assuredly come, when he will bitterly repent his ever having yielded to these temptations, whilst he will not be long in discovering that he has bought a short-lived present gratification at the expense of future pain and misery, to the utter destruction of those gentlemanly and independent feelings which he should ever most studiously cherish. I draw no exaggerated picture, for I speak from experience, and in repeated instances, when I affirm, that this *curse* of debt in India has driven many a man, otherwise the soul of honour, to expedients which have cost him his commission and place in society, or, in other cases, to the desperate means of self-destruction, by trying to drown the recollection of the continued cause of pain in the wine-cup. It is, indeed, one of the faults of the younger branches of the Indian service, that they complain of their inadequate means, whilst they take no pains to adapt their outlay to those means. I do not intend to say, that the pay of an Ensign in India is more than sufficient for the absolute wants of the officer; but it is certainly adequate to those wants, if judiciously employed, and particularly so in field stations. I would instance the officers of Her Majesty's army in India; their allowances are, if any thing, less than those serving in the Company's, yet debt is not only unknown, but strictly discountenanced: it would be well were the same rule rigidly enforced in the latter service also.

The mistake is generally made by young

E

men in India imagining that debts incurred whilst they remain subalterns may be paid off on promotion. This, however, is a vital error; for the rate of compound interest charged by the usurers and panderers to youthful extravagance, precludes the possibility of emancipation from the toils thus around their victim. It will be sufficient to mention, that at the rate of common interest in India, 9 per cent., the original debt is doubled in seven years, and thus long after the actual debt itself may have been defrayed, it is paid over and over again in the shape of interest. This the law allows and enforces; but in the case of money borrowed from shroffs and others, a much higher rate of premium is charged; and as usury laws do not extend to a contract on honour between an officer and a native, the amount must sooner or later be paid. In one word, of all the errors a young man in India can commit at his outset particularly, though the same rule may apply to any portion of his career, few are so fraught with fatal consequences as extravagance and its concomitants; the more dangerous because the more specious and fascinating. Let them be most studiously avoided, even to the minutest particle, at starting, and he will in all probability be safe for the future. If the Cadet be but determined to suit his expenditure to his allowances, he will not only find no difficulty in so doing, but the writer could produce instances of those who have saved money from them. Be this as it may, however, rigid economy must, at least until his promotion to a lieutenancy, be the young officer's leading principle; and he must reflect that, though the thoughtless amongst his companions may try to keep pace with their seniors, they only do so at the cost of involving themselves in ultimate inextricable difficulties; and that he, on the other hand, by making what are, after all, only trifling sacrifices for the present, will be rewarded with that emancipation from difficulties and independence of feeling hereafter, of more value than any amount of present excitement, procured by going beyond his means and incurring debts and obligations. The

above remarks, though addressed to the
young and inexperienced, may be useful to
all, for the evil is one of a common kind in
India; and though, particularly with new
comers, much mischief in the way of unnecessary expenditure, dissipation, and waste
of time, often results from a protracted stay
at the presidencies, the Cadet should, I am
of opinion, be at once sent up the country
to join the regiment to which he stands ap-
pointed, allowing him only just a sufficient
period at the presidency to procure the necessaries for his equipment: by this means
he will avoid what may be considered as a
probable cause of evil, and begin at once to
have his time profitably occupied in learning
his duty, and becoming acquainted with the
language, troops, and service generally. This
rule is now, I am happy to say, acted upon
more than formerly, and to the eminent advantage of the Cadet no less than the public
service. Parents and guardians are often
unwittingly the cause of extravagance in
their charges on their first arrival in India,
from the practice of either giving them

larger sums of money than they can require, or by permitting them credit for such sums as they may please to draw. These are great errors, and should be avoided. The Cadet may be allowed to possess a certain amount for his equipment in India, and this need only be very moderate: Rs. 1,000 or £100, for instance, or even less, will be found ample, to furnish a horse, tent, and all that can possibly be required, fitted out as Cadets are previous to leaving England. On no account should this sum or any other given for a like purpose be allowed to be exceeded, except at the Cadet's own cost and risk; for to place a young man in possession of the means to be extravagant in a country like India, is at least giving him a temptation to which older and more experienced heads might succumb; and those prove themselves his best friends in the end, who teach him at starting to rely solely upon his own resources.

The economy and occupation of time in India are important points, and the Cadet, or young officer, should as soon as possible bring himself into habits of regularity and method in this respect; they will thus adhere to him for the future. In the ordinary outline of cantonment duty, the mornings, from dawn to a short period after sunrise, are appropriated to the parade and exercise of the regiment; that done, the whole of the succeeding portion of the four-and-twenty hours may be said to be completely at the regimental officer's own disposal; if he have staff or other duties to attend to, the case is of course altered.

To profitably fill up this period of time with employment, in a climate so inciting to indolence and lassitude as India, requires, I own, a considerable share of resolution and perseverance; but the difficulty should be met with energy and surmounted at starting, it otherwise obtains the mastery and is seldom to be conquered afterwards; for if no efforts be made to overcome it at once, the evil grows with the continued existence of the cause, and those habits of idleness, with their never-failing companions, are perpetuated, to the loss of the health and advance-

ment of the European in India. In the
commencement of this sketch, I endeavoured
to attract attention to this subject as one of
great importance, and wished to point out
the means to be adopted previous to entering India, for placing the Cadet in possession of objects of study and inquiry, which
shall induce interesting and profitable employment of his time in that country. Leaving these, however, there will be found immediate calls upon the Cadet's attention
when he joins his regiment, and these will
find him enough to do. In the first place
he should devote at least six hours daily to
the language in private study, and with his
moonshee he cannot expect to progress ra-
pidly with less; he must have a considerable
portion of his day devoted to the drill-ser-
geant, and learning the internal economy of
the regiment and his duty generally; the rest
he would do well to fill up by reading, and
by keeping a regular register of all he sees
and hears connected with his own position,
as well as the first impressions made upon
him by the country, its people, and the con-

tinued subjects of novelty and interest about
him. This is not to be considered as a
mere common-place journal, in which the
most vapid and senseless remarks are to
find a place, as is generally the case with
such productions, but should be made a work
of study and reflection. The great advantage of this method of occupying time is in
the habit and facility of expressing opinions
on paper which it begets; and as India is a
field for the constant employment of the
pen in official no less than private and general matters, it is highly desirable to be
able to wield it skilfully and with aptitude.
Of in-door occupation I can say little beyond
what I have already adduced: music, drawing, and resources of all and every kind are
valuable, and to be appreciated as the great
barriers to the mischief which always results
from the absence of such means of passing
time in India. Few who can find pleasant or
profitable employment at home, will seek for
either cards, tiffins, or billiards, though they
are found to be the great sources of *killing
time*, as it is called, in Indian cantonments.

On the subject of the field sports of India, for which that country is so celebrated, I would only wish to caution the young officer against employing them as the business rather than wholesome recreation of life. In the former case they will be found ruinous to his pocket and dangerous to his health; whilst enjoyed in moderation, they are to be encouraged as highly conducive to that spirit and contempt of danger becoming the soldier. " The mode of hunting, which opens the fairest field to valour, may justly be considered as the image and the school of war." And as in India, " the sportsman boldly encounters the wild boar and provokes the fury of the tiger, so where there is danger there may be glory;"* and all the manly field sports of that country, hog hunting, tiger shooting, &c., are commendable to a certain extent, if not allowed to engross too much time and attention. Continued exposure to the sun of India, moreover, though it be little felt under the extraordinary and maddening excitement of the chase, espe-

* Gibbon.

cially by the younger and fresher sportsman,
yet never fails to work its deleterious effect
on his constitution; and as it is impossible
to partake of these sports without braving
the climate to an unusual degree, on that
account he should limit his excursions to
reasonable bounds.   Moreover, highly as such
manly sports may be prized by the young
soldier, they should cease the moment he
finds he is not provided with the means to
keep them up: dogs, hunters, and sporting
establishments in India, as in England, are
expensive, and dip deeply into the pocket;
and though subalterns in India generally keep
a larger stud than field officers, it is needless
to say, that in the former case credit sup-
plies what the allowances will not provide.
As no one can pretend to have any connection with the *turf* in India unless he is a
monied man, or prepared to play a game far
beyond the calculation of a subaltern in the
Honourable Company's army, I shall only
allude to the subject to observe, that I never
yet saw or knew any thing connected with
the *course* in India which I could recom-

mend to the uninitiated; and in my humble
opinion, though the result of experience, it
is not likely at any time to become profitable to the pocket, and may prove dangerous
to the reputation of those who intermeddle
with this very attractive description of gambling.

That much depends on associates, and
that it is important to a young man to look
well to the private characters of his constant companions, or those whom he admits
to his intimacy, all will readily allow, yet
few sufficiently act upon the principle. In
India, society assumes a very high position,
and though in no army can the honour, reputation, and high tone of feeling of its officers be more scrupulously maintained than
in that of the Company, still as this does
not extend to habits of life, tastes, and private character, the Cadet should not hastily
form any but mere acquaintances, such as
are allowed on the footing in which all the
members of society are placed, constituted
like that of the military: beyond this, he
should well study the characters of his friends,

or those whom he proposes to make such; let them be chosen from those whose society is valuable, and there will be no difficulty in finding many such.

The force of example is difficult to resist, and there are those in India, who from habit and association think lightly of much which is otherwise and in reality highly objectionable, and are too apt to instil their own practices and opinions into the new comer, the agent generally being ridicule, and the argument " want of spirit." Let the Cadet, however, be on his guard against the system of " doing so and so because others do it," and keep up as much as he possibly can his European tastes and ideas; they will save him from much which it is necessary he should avoid. I have before pressed upon his attention the vital error of assimilating in any degree, however trifling, to Oriental manners or customs. To this let him scrupulously adhere, and, above all, let no consideration prompt him to form connections with the females of the country, rather let him marry as an Ensign. My remarks on adopting customs will tell with double force on this most destructive and pernicious practice.

With respect to health and climate, I shall confine myself to a few words, since I believe few general rules can be given applicable to all constitutions. There are those who simply recommend attention to what is found to agree with the health, either in diet or mode of living generally, and acting thereon without reference to any other rules or instructions whatever; and certainly from the extraordinary dissimilarity in the effects produced on different constitutions in India by exactly the same causes, I am inclined to agree with this method, and to advise pursuing the ordinary course of living as adopted in India, altering the same, or otherwise, as may be found necessary from the effects produced. There is one rule, however, which is a general one, applicable to all, and which should be rigidly observed too : it is, that the groundwork of preserving health in India is temperance, coupled with regular hours and exercise. There are many who defy it in practice and deny it in theory, but the cases are indeed few where it is done with impunity; and the Cadet may rest assured, that though he may see some of his countrymen in India act totally regardless of this rule, he will not be long in discovering, if he too should attempt to depart from it, how unerring and fatal are its consequences. The medium is the point to be adhered to: the climate requires and nature demands a generous diet and what may be called good living; but once exceed the ordinary and necessary bounds, or give way to irregularity, the European constitution cannot stand it in a tropical climate, and infallibly gives way. Retiring to rest early in India is essential to health, and few species of dissipation have a worse tendency than late hours.

With due attention to the occupation of the mind, regular living, by which I mean regular hours for meals and rest, exercise, and temperance, the climate of India will be found to have few of the terrific qualities so unjustly imputed to it, much being attributed to the climate which results in reality

from the habits and practices of Europeans,
oftentimes amounting to utter recklessness
and a defiance of the commonest rules even
of the natives themselves. I have no reason
to believe from experience, but that, with
ordinary care and attention to his health,
the European in India, under ordinary circumstances, will find the climate have but
trifling effect on his constitution; and in
cases where disease is epidemic and general,
there is still the consolation left, that he is
best able to grapple with the enemy who
shall be found prepared to meet him.

The subject of advice to the Cadet, and general rules for his proceedings in India, might
be extended, but probably with little advantage, since much must depend on strength
of mind, good sense, and use of the faculty
of observation, in a completely novel situation, where the young man finds himself,
probably for the first time in his life, his
own master, and where it rests entirely
with himself to shape out a course which
shall lead to advancement and distinction in
his service, or otherwise. His health, com-

fort, reputation, and, indeed, all that materially and deeply concerns his welfare and
happiness in life, are in his own hands, and
he may make or mar his prospects as he
pleases.   I would not be mistaken, as conveying an idea that India is the " *El Dorado* "
many consider it; nor do I wish to create
false ideas in the minds of those who enter
the Hon. Company's service, by speaking too
highly of that service and its prospects.   In
India, as elsewhere, a public servant must
work, and hard too, to bring himself to notice; he must prove himself in every way
worthy of the confidence of his superiors ere
he is raised above the level of ordinary duties.   India is no longer the field of wealth
and fame it was at the end of the last cen-
tury, and the competition in talent and ca-
pability to be encountered there in the present day draws the wide distinction between
our own and those times, when ordinary
qualifications, even as linguists, never failed
to secure valuable appointments.   A different view was then taken of India and the
Indian military service; it was the "*pis al-*

ler " of younger sons, and often the last resource of those who were considered to be,
or had proved themselves, fit for no other.
Its climate was viewed with terror, and men
braved it as a sort of desperate resource to
amass wealth : now, however, the case is
altered ; we have a superior class of men as
Cadets, whether as respects rank or education, and just conclusions are arrived at as to
India and its openings to those who adopt it.

The fact is, however, that as it at present
stands, there is no comparison to be drawn
between the Company's service and any other
of the present day ; and the Cadet who is
fortunate enough to enter it may congratulate himself, without any extravagant notions
as to his true position, that he has been, in
the first place, provided for for life ; that,
whilst his constitution and energies are un-
impaired, his pay, throughout all the grades
of the service in the ordinary routine of duty,
is on the most liberal scale, as compared to
other military services ; and, when the failure
of health and strength shall interfere to prevent his continuing on active service, there

is secured to him a handsome pension, without reference to the chances of promotion, and the enjoyment of ease and comfort for the rest of his days. In the second place, no service allows of such numerous openings for appointments, independent of ordinary duty, as the large staff of India, chosen entirely from the commissioned ranks of the army, as also in the constitution of Government and administration of authority in a country where political and various other highly important and responsible posts have to be filled up by members of the army. And thirdly, no military service but that of the Hon. Company's, let the capabilities and qualifications of its officers be what they may, so continually presents such opportunities for distinction, either in the field or cabinet; and no government is so liberal and ready to foster and encourage those of its servants who prove themselves, by conduct, talent, zeal, or energy, worthy of the notice of their superiors.

On this head, however, I shall conclude as I began, that all rests with the parties them-

selves; and that exertion, steady perseverance in certain rules of conduct, and a deter-
mination of adapting· the means to the end,
can alone be depended upon for advancement
in India, or for securing the peculiar advantages offered to the European officer in that
country, beyond all other services of the
present day.

FINIS.

Printed by J. L. Cox & Sons, 75, Great Queen Street,
Lincoln's-Inn Fields.

CPSIA information can be obtained at www.ICGtesting.com
Printed in the USA
LVOW05s1110020114

367774LV00009B/83/P